OPTIONS TRADING

HOW TO TRADE FOR A LIVING

7-DAY CRASH COURSE FOR BEGINNERS

SECRET STRATEGIES, TIPS AND TRICKS

MARK STOCK

© Copyright 2019 by Mark Stock
All rights reserved.

The content of this book may not be reproduced, duplicated, or transmitted without direct written permission from the author or the publisher.

Under no circumstances will any blame or legal responsibility be held against the publisher, or author, for any damages, reparation, or monetary loss due to the information contained within this book.

Legal Notice:

This book is copyright protected and is only for personal use. You cannot amend, distribute, sell, use or quote any part of this book without the consent of the author or publisher.

Disclaimer Notice:

Please note the information contained within this document is for educational purposes only. The author of this book is not a registered investment advisor and assumes no responsibility for trading and investment results. Please be aware that trading involves a high degree of risk. All effort has been executed to present accurate, up to date, and reliable information. No warranties of any kind are declared or implied. The strategies and the methods presented in this book are provided for informational and educational purposes and should not be considered as investment advice. Please consult a licensed professional before attempting any techniques described in this guide. By reading this document, the reader agrees that under no circumstances is the author responsible for any losses, direct or indirect, which are incurred as a result of the use of the information contained within this document, including, errors, omissions, or inaccuracies.

Table of Contents

INTRODUCTION 6

CHAPTER 1: AN OVERVIEW OF OPTIONS 8
    What is an option? 9
    Options Expire 10
    Pricing definitions 11
    Most Options Are Not Exercised 12
    Option Price Quotes 12
    Option Lifetime 13
    Writing, Buying, and Selling 13
    Maximum Financial Risk 14
    You Can start with small amounts of capital 15
    Pros and Cons of Options Trading 19
    ROI of Stocks 23
    Trading Levels 27
        Level 1 Trading 27
        Level 2 Trading 28
        Level 3 29
        Level 4 30

CHAPTER 2: OPTIONS BASICS 32
    Call Option 32
    Put Option 32
    Exercising an Option 33
    The Main Reason People Write Options Contracts 33
    Options Chains (or tables) 35
    Strike Price 35
    Expiration Date 38
    Underlying Asset 38
    Summarizing main characteristics of options 39
    Most Options Expire Worthless 39
    Reading an Options Chain 40
    The Broker 46
    The Market Maker 48

CHAPTER 3: HOW OPTIONS PRICES ARE DETERMINED 50
- In the Money 52
- Out of the Money 54
- How this works for Put Options 56
- Price of the Underlying 57
- Extrinsic or Time Value 60
- Time Decay 62
- Implied Volatility 63
- How many options are exercised 64

CHAPTER 4: THE GREEKS 66
- Delta 66
- Gamma 73
- Theta 74
- Vega 76
- Rho 78

CHAPTER 5: OPTIONS ON INDEX FUNDS 80

CHAPTER 6: WRITING OPTIONS AND EARNED INCOME 91
- Covered Calls 92
- Naked Call 98
- Naked Puts 100
- Times when naked strategies could work 102

CHAPTER 7: OPTIONS STRATEGIES 103
- Strangles 103
- Straddles 104
- Selling covered calls against LEAPS and other LEAPS Strategies 105
- Buying Put Options as Insurance 106
- Spreads 107
- Iron Condor 110
- Iron Butterfly 111

CONCLUSIONS 113

Introduction

Welcome and congratulations on purchasing this exciting book!

This guide will introduce the concept of options, explain how they work, and how you can invest in them and earn profits.

Unfortunately, the world of options is full of a lot of technical jargon. Our goal is to cut through all of that and explain how options work in plain English. We will show you exactly what you need to do in order to trade options and earn money. But first, why would you want to trade options rather than invest in stocks?

Options are exciting for three reasons. The first is you don't have to invest a large amount of money. You can start buying options for as little as $100, or even $50. As you get better at trading, you can increase your investments and earn even bigger profits. Owning 100 shares of most stocks would cost you thousands to tens of thousands of dollars or more. While you would have to put up $20,000 to own 100 shares of Apple, you can buy an option poised to make solid profits for $100.

Second, the potential return on investment (ROI) for options is much larger than what you can achieve when trading stocks. We will demonstrate this with specific examples, and the numbers are jaw-dropping.

Finally, options are (usually) short-lived financial instruments. That can work against you, but it also means you can earn profits quickly. While there are long term options available, with most options you are going to get in and out quickly.
There is an added bonus – with options you can make money no matter which direction the stock is heading. In order to short stocks, you need to have a large margin account. With options, instead, this can be done for a small sum of money.

So hopefully you are excited about options! Keep in mind that this book is no claim or guarantee that you will make any money off of any investments that you make. Any reader of this book makes investments at their own risk, and if uncertain about what to do, you should always consult a financial advisor. While we attempt to be as realistic as possible in this book, any examples provided herein are for educational purposes only. Finally, with any investments you make, you do so at your own risk. Remember that all investment activities come with a risk of loss of capital.

With that out of the way, let's get started!

Chapter 1: An Overview of Options

Options offer an exciting way for investors to get involved in *trading*. Trading is different than long-term or "buy and hold" investing. Rather than investing in companies in order to build your wealth over a long time period, trading is a method based on using the price movements of securities to earn profits. Most traders seek to earn profits in the near term, the most famous trading method is day trading. In that case, traders open and close their positions within a single trading day.

Trading is often viewed by the public as "gambling". But that perception is not realistic. Traders spend a great deal of time studying the markets, including looking at the fundamentals of the companies they invest in and using technical tools to forecast future price movements. There is a certain probability of success with different trades, but that does not compare to gambling, it is not like spinning a slot machine and hoping lady luck smiles on you. You are not going to be making random options purchases.

The word "trading" can be a loaded term. I will use trading and investing interchangeably because in my view many of the differences are technicalities. You invest to make money, therefore saying that you are investing in options is a perfectly reasonable way to express it.

In this chapter we will begin by giving a formal definition of what an option is. Then we will get into some specifics that you need to know before you start trading.

What is an option?

An option is a contract based on 100 underlying shares of stock. Each contract fixes the price of the stock at a value called the *strike price*. Options also expire, they come with an expiration date which is sometimes referred to as the *expiry*.

There are two types of options. These are known as *call options* and *put options*. A call option gives the buyer the right to buy 100 shares of stock at the strike price. The contract is called an "option" because buying the shares is optional for the buyer. This is advantageous for the buyer if the market price of the stock rises above the strike price. That way they could save money by being able to get the shares at a discount. This is where an option gets its value.

The higher the market price, the more valuable the option becomes. Of course, if the strike price is above the market price, a call option is not worth nearly as much. But if the share price rises, they will gain in value.

A put option gives the buyer the right to *sell* 100 shares of stock at the strike price. So, a put option is a contract that gets its value from declining share prices. The way this works is that the investor buys a put option if they believe that future market prices will decline. This fixes the price of the shares. If prices drop by a large amount, they can buy the shares on the open market, and then sell them to the originator of the options contract at the strike price. Since the strike price is higher than the market price, the investor has made a profit.

Options Expire

It is important to focus on the fact that options expire. Time works against an option: the less time on the contract, the lower the probability that market prices will move in the options' favor. This characteristic of options is known as *time decay.*

If a call option reaches the expiration date and its strike price is below the market price, it could be *exercised*, which means the owner of the option could buy the 100 shares of stock. This has two advantages. The stock could be immediately sold at the higher market price, earning the investor a profit. Alternatively, if they actually wanted to own the stock, the option gave them the ability to get the shares at a discounted price.

If the strike price is above the market price at that point, the option is worthless, because there would be no point in buying shares of stock at a higher price. In the industry, they say the *option expires worthless.*

For a put option, on the date of expiration, it's considered valuable if the strike price is above the market price. In that case, the investor can exercise the option by selling the shares of stock at a price that is higher than the market price, earning a profit.

Put options can also be used in an alternative way. Some investors that hold a large number of shares may buy put options as a form of insurance. This can protect them from a catastrophic loss if the stock undergoes a significant decline in price. A put option provides a safety valve they can use to protect their shares.

If the strike price of a put option is below the market price, it expires worthless. An investor is not going to opt to sell shares when they would sell for less than market price.

Pricing definitions

The relationship between option price and market price falls into one of three categories. These are:

- At the money: this means the option strike price is exactly equal to the share price.
- In the money: this means the strike price is favorable with respect to the market price. For a call option, that

means the strike price is below the market price. For a put option, that means the strike price is above the market price.

- Out of the money: this means the strike price is unfavorably positioned. For a call option, that means that the strike price is above the market price. For a put option, that means the strike price is below the market price.

Most Options Are Not Exercised

About 85% of options expire worthless. The exact number quoted varies, but the only thing you need to know is that three quarters, or more, of options expire worthless.

There is some mythology about this – people think that because most options expire worthless, they are not exercised. In fact, if an option is in the money the probability that it will be exercised is non-trivial. It constitutes a risk only if you are the originator of the contract. As a trader of options, someone who is buying and selling them on the market, that is not of concern.

Option Price Quotes

Options are quoted on a per-share basis. Therefore, you will see an option price listed as $0.74, although that is not the actual price that you will pay for the option. This is a per share quote, and most options cover 100 shares of stock. The actual price that you will pay for an option is the quoted price x 100. In this case, that would be $0.74 x 100 = $74.

Option Lifetime

As a general standard, options last a month. Options typically expire every Friday, but some expire on Wednesdays. There are also weekly options that expire within one week of issue. You can also get long term options that last anywhere between several weeks to 1-2 years. If they last a year or longer, they are called *LEAPS*, which stands for Long-term Equity Anticipation Security. All options have the same characteristics and behave in the same way, the only difference between them is the length of time to the expiration date.

Writing, Buying, and Selling

Many beginners get confused by the different roles that traders can play in the market. Most investors involved in options are simply *trading*. This means that you *buy* an options contract to open your position. You can choose to buy a call option, a put option, or a combination of call and put options. When you buy an option contract you have no obligations under the option, and you are free to sell them to others. In the same way, on the stock market, you don't actually make a deal with someone to sell your option, you simply place an order through your broker, and they handle it for you. Traders buy and sell options hoping to make profits from the transactions as the share price moves up and down. If you get stuck with an option that is out of the money and close to expiration, you are out of luck at that point and it will probably expire worthless.

You can also *sell to open*. For example, you will be obligated to if the option is exercised by the buyer. Using industry jargon, we say that you have been *assigned*. They say you are a "writer", but you don't actually write a contract as an individual investor. You simply get on your brokerage contract, and you find existing options for a given stock. When you find one you like, you place an order to *sell it* through your broker. People sell options because they can earn a monthly income by doing so, even though selling comes with some risks.

Maximum Financial Risk

If you buy options, the maximum risk to you is the money you paid to buy the option. So, if you buy an option for $100 your risk is $100.

If you sell call options, the risk is that you will have to sell the 100 shares of stock. If you own the stock the risk is that you will lose the shares. If you don't already own the stock, then you face financial risk. The risk per share is the difference in price between the market price and the share price.

If you sell put options, the risk is that you will have to buy the shares at the strike price. So, your total risk is the strike price x 100 shares. That is the absolute financial risk, of course you might be stuck with shares of stock that are worthless. As we will see, there are ways to protect yourself from having to buy the stock.

You Can start with small amounts of capital

One of the benefits of options trading is that you can begin investing with small amounts of money. You can even do it with $10, $50 or $100. Options on the most popular stocks that are trading at high prices will cost more, but in comparison to share price they are much cheaper. It can help if we look at some real-life examples. Keep in mind that with these examples, and any others throughout the book, all prices quoted are the prices at the time of writing and are subject to change.

The first stock that we are going to look at is Advanced Micro Devices, which trades under the ticker AMD. On today's date it is priced at $32.41 a share. Keep that money number in mind as we look at some of the options contracts that are available for the stock. To buy 100 shares of AMD it would cost $3,241.

When buying an option, remember that if you think the price of the stock is going to rise between the present date and the expiration date of the option, you buy a call option. If you think the price is going to decline between the present date and the expiration date, you buy a put option.

We can check call options for AMD by logging into our brokerage account. There are multiple expiration dates available, and the specific options available may vary depending on what broker you are using. At the time of writing, there are options expiring every Friday in July and August, with some long-term options with expiration dates sprinkled throughout fall and also including January 17, 2020, June 19, 2020, January 15, 2021, and March 19, 2021.

When buying an option, you want to buy options that have an expiration date at least 2-3 weeks ahead, so that you have enough time for the stock price to rise or fall as needed. If there are big news such as an earnings call or major announcement coming up, you might be able to buy an option that expires in a week and still earn profits.

The longer the time to expiration, the higher the price. Let us look at some specifics. First, focusing on two weeks to expiration, a call option for AMD with a $31.50 strike price is quoted at $0.94. Therefore, in order for me to buy it I would have to spend $0.94 x 100 = $94.

An option with the same strike price that expires a week later is $1.55 – so the total price would be $155. A LEAP expiring in a year and a half is much more expensive – it would cost $800. There are some advantages to buying LEAPS, and we will discuss those later.

Now let's compare put options prices. Remember, you will buy a put option if you think that AMD will decline in price. The put option for the same $31.50 strike price that expires in two weeks is listed at $1.22. A week later, the same strike price would cost $1.81. A LEAP would be $7.80 per share.

You will notice that the near-term put options are more expensive. The reason is simple. The share price of AMD has declined recently, and this indicates investors are expecting more declines.

To see how prices vary with strike price, let's focus on a particular date. This time I will look at IBM, and we will focus on options that expire in three weeks. First, we will look at call options.

IBM is more valuable than AMD, so the options are going to be more expensive. The share price of IBM is currently $141.54.

Considering call options, those that are in the money are worth more. An option with a strike price of $141, which is barely "in the money", is $4.10 per share. Compare that to one that is $5 in the money. An option with a strike price of $136 is $7.43. Another one with a strike price of $120 is $22.43.

In contrast, out of the money options are cheaper. A $146 call would cost $1.77, and a $150 call is $0.74 per share. Keep in mind that as long as you are not too close to the expiration date, out of the money options can increase in value, and earn profits. In fact, the $146 call increased in value by 33.49% in a single day, because the share price of IBM increased.

Out of the money, options are cheaper, so they offer a way to make profits with a lower up-front investment. However, they can be tricky: if the share price drops, they can lose value fast.

Since IBM has gained value recently, the put options have lost value. A $141 put option is priced at $3.45, which is lower than the price quoted for the call option that has the same strike price ($4.10 per share).

Remember that IBM is $141.54 a share. To buy 100 shares, it would cost you $14,154. In comparison, buying the $141 option expiring in three weeks would cost $410. And as we will see, if the share price goes up, the ROI on the option is going to be far higher than it would be on the stock.

Pros and Cons of Options Trading

Just like anything else, there are pros and cons that come with trading options. The concept sounds great, and in my opinion it is, but options carry risks as well as rewards. It's important to be familiar with both.

First, let's review the advantages. As we have noted, options allow you to get in the market with a far lower amount of capital up-front. If you actually buy shares of stock, it can cost you 20-50 times as much as an options contract would cost.

The second advantage is that options can earn you a much higher return on your investment. Let's say you are a "swing trader", which is someone that buys stock with the hope of earning a profit on a price swing over a short time period. If you buy 100 shares of IBM at $141 a share and the price of the stock goes up by $3 a share, when you close your position you have made $300 profit, minus commissions. Your initial investment would be $14,100. On the other hand, if you buy an option, you can invest $410 and earn a profit of $150. So, you could have made the same $300 profit in absolute terms buying two options, only having to put $820 up-front. You can do the maths to find out how much profit you would make if you put the same amount of money into both investments. On many trading platforms, options trade commission-free.

Another advantage of options is the expiration date, although it is also a liability. Options are a way to make money quickly. You get in, and you get out of your investments.

Options offer leverage. For each options contract you buy, you control 100 shares of stock without actually owning them.

If you buy shares of stock, you benefit if the price rises. You have probably heard about people "shorting" the market, but when it comes to stocks these are big players that have large margin accounts. They have powers that ordinary investors simply don't have, so taking advantage of price declines in the market is not usually something available to small investors. However, as we noted earlier, put options give you that power. You can short the market for as little as $50 or $100.

Options traders can also create setups that earn profits no matter which direction the stock price moves. That is something you definitely cannot do by owning stocks. We will explain the details in a later chapter.

Finally, you can invest in options risking small amounts of capital. That way if you are on the losing end of your trade, the amount of money you lose is fixed and known beforehand.

So, these are the main advantages you get investing in options. If there were no negative sides to it, everyone would be investing in options and becoming millionaires. The reality is options trading can be tricky, and if you don't do it right you will just lose money.

The first disadvantage is that options prices can move fast. The price of an option can double or triple over the course of a couple of hours, and it can also decrease over a short time span. If you are not paying close attention to your trades, you might lose an opportunity to make profits or find yourself with losses in the blink of an eye. In my early trading days, I experienced both outcomes.

Secondly, while the expiration date can be a positive, it is also a major risk factor. One mistake beginners make is not paying attention to the expiration date. If an option is out of the money, it can lose value extremely quickly in the days leading up to expiration. If you are not paying attention and fail to get out of the trade, you can find that prices drop so fast it is not worth bothering.

The next disadvantage is options training can be complicated. I don't recommend just diving in to see what happens. You need to educate yourself before you start trading: start with small trades so that you learn the ropes without investing a large amount of capital. The concept of put options is a little bit foreign to most people, so it should be studied before you start buying.

Finally, I would like to point out that due to the time limit and rapid price movements, options can entrap people who are susceptible to getting overly emotional about investing. This can happen in a couple of different ways. If you are seeing prices rise, you might check your trades and find that an option you bought for $100 has suddenly tripled in value. The smart trader would immediately sell and take the profit. But far too many people get excited, exuberant, or greedy – however, you want to put it. They forget that the option can rapidly deteriorate because of time decay or a turn in market prices, and they hold on to it for too long and, a day or two later, they are in a losing position.

The second problem is panic. An investor prone to panic is not suitable to getting involved with options trading. We will talk more about the details later, but a $1 change in share price can cause a change in option price by $50 or $100. If you are talking about something like Apple that is $200 a share, a $1 change in share price is a small move – but that can have a big impact on the price of the option depending on multiple factors. Do you have enough mettle to watch the option lose $75 in a few minutes, stick to your fundamentals and wait for prices to rise? Many beginners panic and then exit their positions prematurely.

ROI of Stocks

One of the main reasons for people to trade options, as opposed to buying stocks, is commonly referred to as ROI, or return on investment. The fact is that the ROI on options is far larger than the ROI on stocks. Let's create an example to illustrate the difference in profit margins.

For this example, we will use a call option. We will also assume that it is now 21 days before the option expires. Considering a stock that is trading at $50 a share, we will buy an at the money call option. Since it is at the money, the share price is the same as the strike price, at $50.

In this case, the quote on the option will be $0.96. This means the actual price is $0.96 x 100 = $96 to buy the option.

Considering that at $50 a share, an investment in 100 shares would cost $5,000, a price of $96 to control the shares for three weeks seems like a good deal. Should the investment not work out for us, we have also capped our total loss at $96.

Now, suppose that seven days have passed, so we have 14 days to expiration. If the price of the stock rises to $53 a share the value of an investment in the stock has increased from $5,000 to $5,300 – a gain of $300.

Let us compare this to an option on the stock. At 14 days to option expiration, if the share price rises to $53 the price of the option on a per share basis has increased to $3.07, for a total of $307 for the option. If we sold the option at this point, that would be a gross profit of $211. Also, there are many brokerages that have commission-free option trading, so in many cases that is your profit, period.

Now, let's compare the ROI or return on investment in both cases. If you are not familiar with it the formula for ROI is:

ROI = (Value of investment now – initial cost of investment)/(initial cost of investment)

It is expressed as a percentage. Let's go ahead and look at our hypothetical investment in the stock.

- Initial cost of investment equals $5000
- Value of investment now equals $5300
- Value of investment now − initial cost of investment = $5300 -$5000 = $300

Now we can plug this into the ROI formula (I am going to multiply by 100 in order to express this as the percentage):

ROI = $300/$5000 x 100 = 6%

Under normal circumstances, a 6% return would be considered respectable, especially over a week period. That is why many people engage in swing trading.

Now for comparison, let's take a look at the options contract that we have been considering. The initial cost of investment was just $96, and to refresh your memory, we sold it for $307.

So, in the case of the option, this is what we have:

- The initial cost of investment equals $96
- Value of investment now equals $307
- Value of investment now - initial cost of investment = $307 - $96 = $211

Now we will take those values and put them into the ROI formula. This is what we get in the case of the option:

ROI = $211/$96 x 100 = 2.198 x 100 = 219.8%

The ROI for the option is far larger. This is a typical result, and, for many, it is a convincing enough argument that options trading is a good way to get involved in trading, as compared to swing or day trading.

Let's take another example. Let's say we have IBM at $141 a share. A swing trader buys 100 shares for $14,100 hoping to make a profit. But, unfortunately, 5 days later IBM's CEO is unexpectedly arrested for committing crimes, and the share price drops to $132 a share. The swing trader unloads their shares at a loss of $9 a share. Their total loss is $900.

A smart options investor bought a put and a call on the same day, with a $140 strike price on the call and a $137 strike price on the put. The call cost $4.00 and the put cost $1.78, for a total cost of $578. Five days later, when the bad news hit, the price drop to $132 hurts the call option significantly but benefits the put option.

The price of the call drops to $0.51. The options trader immediately sells it to recover the $51. However, the put option rises to $8.50. The options trader sells the put for $850, so they end up with a total of $901, for a net profit of $323.

Admittedly, this is a somewhat contrived example – but it shows how options trading allows you to do things ordinary stock trading does not. Later we will learn specific methods professional options traders have developed to minimize losses and increase the odds of profits. You can use these methods to profit no matter which direction the stock goes, or even profit from situations where the stock hardly moves at all.

Trading Levels

Before you start thinking about trading options, you need to be aware that brokerages classify options traders by level. Since options trading is a bit tricky and carries some risk, brokerages don't just allow you to do anything up-front. The level you are assigned determines what types of trades you are allowed to take part in. Specific details may vary from broker to broker, but they tend to follow the same rules.

Level 1 Trading

The first level is very restrictive, in fact, it only allows you to sell to open options contracts under strict conditions. In the first case, you can do what is known as a *covered call*. This means you are going to sell a call option that is *covered*, meaning it is backed by 100 shares of stock. In other words, you have to own the shares of stock before you can sell a covered call. As we will see, many people who own shares of stock use covered calls to earn monthly income from their investments.

Level 1 traders can also sell to open a *protected put*. A protected put is an option that is backed by the cash needed to buy the shares of stock should the option get exercised. While a protected put has the benefit of providing financial security should the option be exercised, it requires a large amount of capital in your account. It turns out there are other ways to sell puts with relatively low risk, so it's hard to imagine many people selling protected puts.

Level 1 options traders cannot buy options, and they cannot trade options (that is buy an option, and then sell it for a profit).

Level 2 Trading

A level 2 trader can sell covered calls and protected puts. In addition, a level 2 trader can buy calls and puts and trade them on the market. Level 2 traders cannot engage in advanced trading techniques like spreads. Moreover, they are not officially allowed to enter into strangles and straddles, although they can do them indirectly by purchasing options on an individual basis.

Most readers are probably hoping to be at least a level 2 trader. Becoming a level 2 trader requires you to submit to an interview process by the broker. The good news is that the "interview" is done via computer these days, and it is pretty easy to get approval as long as you know what to say. The two main things you need to be aware of before undergoing the interview is that the broker will want to know your investment goals and time horizons. Your answers will need to assure the broker that you understand how options work.

Firstly, they are going to ask you if your goals are long-term capital appreciation or short-term profits. Even if you have a stock portfolio or IRA you are managing for your retirement, you need to tell the broker your investment goal is to make short term profits. Secondly, they are going to ask if you are interested in speculating or investing. You need to tell them that you are interested in speculating. That means that you are buying financial securities with the hopes of selling them for a profit in 1 year or less. Again, what your real goals are overall is not important - you need to tell the broker what they want to hear if you are planning on trading options.

Level 3

If you have not done any options trading, you are probably going to have to spend a few months at level 2 and buy and sell some options before you are approved for level 3. Level 3 opens up some new possibilities for you. As a level 3 trader, most brokerages are going to allow you to engage in certain options strategies that help minimize risk and increase the odds of profit. You will be able to sell options even without cash or owning the stock – as part of one of the pre-defined strategies. The strategies that level 3 traders can use include credit and debit spreads, straddles, strangles, and more complicated trades like an iron condor. Some of these strategies involve the simultaneous sale and purchase of options, and they can even involve call and put options simultaneously. Many brokers set them up for you and will give you the estimated profit and loss in each case.

Level 4

Level 4 is the highest trading level at most brokerages. This allows you to engage in any type of options trading, including selling "naked". This means that you can sell options which are not backed by any cash or collateral. However, that is not strictly accurate, as brokerages require a margin account to engage in that type of trading. In order to open a margin account, you must deposit $2,000 cash. Then, the broker uses a formula to determine the fraction of capital you must have in your account to cover a trade. Keep in mind the money is never spent, it is kept in the account as insurance. While a "protected put" might require you to put $10,000 in your account, for a "naked put" you might only need $1,500. The specifics depend on the specific strike price, underlying stock and other conditions.

Level 4 traders also have access to more advanced trading strategies. These include using multiple legs and special strategies such as a "butterfly" or iron butterfly.

Each additional level of trading gives access to anything a lower level trader can do, so a level 3 trader also has the powers of a level 1 and level 2 trader. For junior traders, it is best to trade some options in a straightforward manner at level 2, before moving up to advanced levels.

Chapter 2: Options Basics

In this chapter, we are going to talk more about the details of options. We are also going to learn all of the jargon that is associated with the options markets and learn how to find options to trade.

Call Option

We have already discussed a little bit about what call options are. But let's give a more formal definition. If you opt to purchase a call option, you are essentially purchasing the opportunity to buy 100 shares of the stock at a fixed price. We will see in chapter 5 why people would want to write a call options contract, but that is not really our concern at this point. So, all you need to do is remember that a call option is a specific opportunity for you to purchase 100 shares of stock. Also, the value of call options goes up as share price rises.

Put Option

This option is the opposite of the call option, in that it seeks to profit from a decline in share price. The buyer of a put option has the right to sell 100 shares of stock at the strike price. If the price of shares drops below the strike price, the buyer is at a distinct advantage. They can buy shares on the option market and then sell them at the higher strike price. The value of put options increases if share price declines.

Exercising an Option

If the buyer of an option exercises their right to buy the shares, we say that they are exercising their right. The seller of the option is then "assigned", that is they are under assignment to sell the shares.

For a put option we say the buyer of the option is exercising their right if they sell the shares to the originator of the contract. Once again, the seller of the option would be assigned.

There are two styles of options. An American style option is one that can be exercised on or before the expiration date of the option. A European style option is one that can only be exercised on the expiration date.

The Main Reason People Write Options Contracts

You can enter into an options contract by logging into your brokerage and selling the options contract to open your position. The reason that you would do this is that you can sell an options contract for a fee which is called the premium. When you sell an options contract to enter a position, you get to keep the premium as profit no matter what happens. In a nutshell, this is the reason why people sell options contracts - to generate monthly income.

There are some risks involved in doing so. If you sell a call contract, the risk is that you are going to have to sell the underlying shares. So, for example, if you own 100 shares of IBM and open a call contract on those shares, the risk is that you will have to sell the shares.

Someone who was using this strategy would probably be hoping that they could profit by selling the options contract to use as a source of monthly income, while keeping the shares. A common strategy is doing it right to be able to sell another options contract the following month. This way you would be able to make some more income from the premium. That works most of the time, but sometimes it is not going to work. If the share price rises above the strike price you selected, you could be assigned and have to sell the shares.

People sell put options for the same reason – to earn monthly income. When you sell a put contract, the risk is that you will have to buy the stock and do so at a high price. So, if someone exercises the contract, you better have access to cash in order to purchase the 100 shares of stock behind the contract.
In most circumstances, the option is never going to be exercised, which is what people are counting on when making put contracts. This way, they basically earn money by selling the put option contract which really is based on nothing. Actually, that is not entirely true. A seller of a put contract is making money

on the risk that they are taking by setting up the contract. That is, they assume the risk from someone else. It could be interpreted as someone buying "insurance" on their stock.

Of course, depending on the amount of cash that you need to come up with to purchase stock, the risk could be significant. The real risk is determined by how much the stock has dropped. So at least there is a lower limit to it.

Options Chains (or tables)

These are just lists of options that can be bought or sold. They are grouped by date and then sorted by price. Call and put options are separated or displayed side by side.

Strike Price

One of the most important characteristics of an options contract is called the *strike price*. The strike price is simply the price the shares of stock would be bought or sold for if the option contract was actually exercised. The relationship between the price of the shares on the market and the strike price will determine, in part, the price of the option if it is traded. The strike value is one of the most critical things that you need to look at. When you open up options tables you are going to find that they are listed in order by the strike price for each date. We already saw that when we looked at AMD prices for options on Robin Hood.

When we look at the options for Apple, we see that they are listed in terms of strike price on the left-hand side. You cannot see that below in this screenshot (it is black because it's after hours). The share price is shown at the center of the screen, which is $194.22. The prices on the left-hand side, which denote that the options are calls, are the strike prices.

The price in the box or inside the button on the right-hand side is the price of the actual options contract. You can see that some other information is provided, such as how much the price went up or down today (these look pretty good for Apple, you can see that some gained 30% or more), as well as the percent change needed to get to break even. Break-even is the price that the option must attain in order for you to have no net profit or loss. This will be the strike price plus the price paid for the option for a call, or the strike price minus the price paid for the option for a put.

The strike price of an option never changes. It is set when the options contract is written or sold for the first time. So, if you see an option for Apple that has a strike price of a $193, that strike price remains the same until the option expires, in which case the option no longer exists. So, remember that it is just a fixed quantity, which is a permanent feature of the options contract. Also remember that the strike price and its relationship with the market price is going to be the central factor in determining whether or not the option can be sold at a profit.

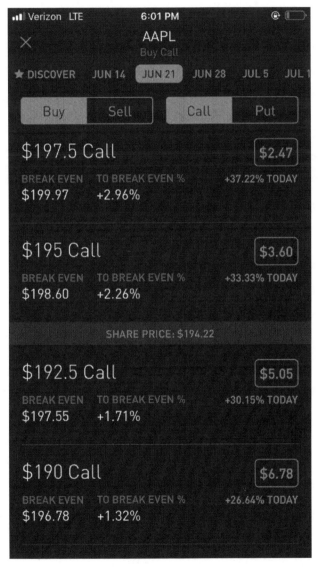

Picture 1

So just to give a specific example, let's look at the option that is right below the line where the share prices are listed. The strike price is $192.50. This means if you owned this option and decided to exercise it, you could purchase the shares of stock at $192.50 a share. That would be true even though the market price or share price of the stock is $194.22.

On the right-hand side, we can see that the quote for the amount of the option is $5.05. This means that you would have to pay $505 to buy one options contract with the strike price of $192.50. The $190 call would cost you $678 to buy.

Expiration Date

The expiration date of the option, just like the strike price, is a fixed quantity as far as the option is concerned. The expiration does not change, and if the option is not exercised on or before the date of its expiration – the option will expire worthless.

Underlying Asset

As per our discussions so far, every options contract has an *underlying*, which is the shares of stock that the options contract controls or represents. So, using the above image as a reference, we listed options contracts for Apple. For each of those, the underlying is 100 shares of Apple stock.

Summarizing main characteristics of options

The main characteristics of the options are the following:

- Call or Put: what type of option is it? If it is a call you have the right to buy 100 shares of the underlying stock at the strike price. All other things being equal, a call option goes up in value if the share price rises. If the price of a stock drops the price of a put option rises (all other things being equal). As you can see, every movement – whether it is upward or downward affects the value of stocks.
- The underlying: this is the asset that backs the option, it is 100 shares of the stock per option contract.
- Strike price: the pre-agreed upon price per share for the stock that underlies the option. If it is a call option, the writer of the contract must sell you the shares at the strike price. If it is a put option, the writer of the contract must purchase the shares at the strike amount.
- Expiration Date: the date the option expires, afterward, it will be worthless and forgotten.

Most Options Expire Worthless

While there is a lot of discussion about the context of options, the vast majority of options contracts, close to 85% on the total, expire worthless. Most options traders are simply hoping to make a profit by buying and selling the options contracts themselves. Even so, if you are going to write options contracts, you do need to be aware that sometimes they do get exercised. In fact, if they expire in the money the broker can exercise them automatically. So, you will need to prepare yourself for that possibility. If you are simply trading options and not writing them, that won't be your concern. There are certain reasons why people would buy options contracts with the hope of buying or selling shares, and we will discuss those. However, most people are not doing options trading for those reasons.

Reading an Options Chain

One of the nice features of newer brokerages like Robin Hood is they make finding an option pretty straightforward. They have basically created an interface that we might call options tables for dummies. However, not all of them are like that, so we should know how to read an option ticker that you find in an options table. Sometimes a listing of options for a given stock like Microsoft, Tesla, or Apple, is called an options chain. An options chain is basically a table listing all the options into sections. One section will include calls, while the other one will include puts. These are grouped together by expiration date. For example, to find options on Yahoo finance, you can look up a given stock ticker and then click on the options tab. So, let's say that I pull up Microsoft. It will bring up the table shown below.

Contract Name	Last Trade Date	Strike	Last Price	Bid	Ask	Change	% Change	Volume	Open Interest	Implied Volatility
MSFT190614C00080000	2019-06-11 10:46AM EDT	90.00	42.32	42.00	42.15	-1.02	-2.35%	1	2	177.34%
MSFT190614C00100000	2019-06-11 11:24AM EDT	100.00	32.24	32.00	32.10	-0.86	-2.60%	5	314	50.00%
MSFT190614C00105000	2019-06-11 3:25PM EDT	105.00	26.85	27.05	27.15	+0.20	+0.75%	15	18	50.00%
MSFT190614C00107000	2019-06-07 10:48AM EDT	107.00	24.80	25.05	25.20	0.00	-	20	48	95.31%
MSFT190614C00108000	2019-06-07 12:10PM EDT	108.00	23.60	24.00	24.25	0.00	-	44	117	91.41%
MSFT190614C00110000	2019-06-11 1:40PM EDT	110.00	21.45	22.05	22.25	-1.95	-8.33%	20	47	92.19%
MSFT190614C00112000	2019-06-11 3:15PM EDT	112.00	19.80	20.05	20.20	-1.85	-8.55%	20	82	76.56%
MSFT190614C00113000	2019-06-11 12:24PM EDT	113.00	18.75	19.05	19.25	-1.90	-9.20%	12	23	80.08%
MSFT190614C00114000	2019-06-10 2:32PM EDT	114.00	19.15	18.05	18.10	0.00	-	19	53	50.00%
MSFT190614C00115000	2019-06-11 10:24AM EDT	115.00	18.15	17.05	17.25	+0.50	+2.83%	11	387	72.27%
MSFT190614C00116000	2019-06-06 3:55PM EDT	116.00	11.70	15.95	16.45	0.00	-	46	57	76.17%
MSFT190614C00117000	2019-06-07 12:03PM EDT	117.00	14.55	14.95	15.30	0.00	-	1	125	58.59%
MSFT190614C00118000	2019-06-10 2:03PM EDT	118.00	15.25	14.05	14.30	0.00	-	11	80	64.45%
MSFT190614C00119000	2019-06-11 3:09PM EDT	119.00	12.85	13.05	13.20	+1.10	+9.36%	1	226	51.17%

Picture 2

As you can see at the top and it tells us the expiration date for the options. Several bits of information are listed from left to right; like stocks, options have their own tickers. These are shown in the far-left column. Each ticker contains valuable information. If you can read the tickers you can basically know what you need to know about the option. Let's take one as an example. We will use the bottom one in the table, which is this one.

MSFT190614C00119000

Obviously, the leading string of characters is the stock ticker for the underlying stock, in this case it is Microsoft. Next, we see a string of numbers which ends right before the C. So, firstly you have the two-digit identification of the year, which in this case is 2019. You need to know the year because there are some options that expire one and two years into the future. Secondly, you have the two-digit identification of the month, which in the example shown here is 06, namely June. The next two digits identify the day of the expiration. In this case, it is 14, so what this tells us is that the option expires on June 14, 2019.

If you see a ticker for an option, you definitely want to pay attention to the letter in the middle. In this case, it is a C, which tells us that this is a call option. If there was a P there, that would mean it was a put option. The last part of the string gives you the strike price of the option. It gives three places for the decimal so, although it says:

119000

what that means is really $119. Remember that the strike price is not the price of the option, which is the price that would be paid per-share if the option were exercised. In this case, the writer of the contract would be required to sell you the shares at $119 per share if the option was exercised.

So, the options ticker provides us with information about the permanent characteristics of the option, or what tells us the underlying, the expiration date, the type of option and strike value. It also has a lot of changing characteristics that we have to read from the table by moving across it left to right. This may be a bit confusing as you are at the first stages of learning, however, with a lot of exposure, you will be able to work through all this data in a breeze soon enough.

Furthermore, if you look at the first column, this shows you the last time the option was traded. Next, we see the strike price: in our example, it is $119. Next to the strike price, we see the most recent price that was used for trading the option. So, this is basically its current value. Here it says $12.85. Remember that there are 100 shares underlined in the option. Therefore, the price for this option is $1285.

Next, we see two columns to the right with more prices. The first one is the *bid*, and the second one is the *ask*. Bid and ask tell you the values that people are willing to pay or accept for the sale of this option. In checking the bid for our example, we can see that the price is $13.05. That tells you that traders are *offering* $13.05 for the option. Again, that is a per-share quote, so the actual price is $1305.

Ask is the current asking price that traders, who are trying to sell the option, are trying to get. In this case, it is $13.20, which is quite a bit more than the bid - so it might take them a while to actually close a sale. If you owned this option, and wanted to sell it quickly, you could sell it for the price at $13.05 or below. If you go with the ask price, you might have to wait.

Next, the table tells you how much the price of the option changed during the day, and then this is followed by the price change in percentage terms. So, this option gained $1.10 for the day, which was an increase of 9.36%.

Volume tells you the number of contracts that were bought or sold that trading day. So, in this case, there is only one contract. That is not a very interesting option since it is not trading very much.

Moving to the right, the next column is open interest. That tells you how many contracts there are in reality, that have not been exercised: these are active positions. In this case, the number listed is 226. So, there are 226 options contracts with this strike price and expiration date that have not been exercised.

The final column is *implied volatility*, and it gets quoted as a percentage. Implied volatility tells you the expected volatility of the stock between the present date and the expiration of the options contract. If the option price is increasing the implied volatility will be large. So, looking at the table, consider the option with the strike price of $90. The implied volatility for that one is 177.34%. On the other hand, looking at the option with the strike price of $119 is much closer to share price, while implied volatility is lower at 51.17%. That is actually fairly high as well.

If you are not familiar with volatility, it is simply defined by how rapidly and by how much the price of the stock changes over time. So, a stock which is changing a lot every single day has high volatility. In contrast, an older stock that is more stable, say like Walgreens, is going to have lower volatility. You can visualize volatility by imagining that a smooth straight line is of low volatility, while one over the same time period that zigzags a lot and goes up and down a lot, is one with high volatility.

All other things being equal, an option with high implied volatility is going to be priced higher than the same option with low implied volatility. You want higher implied volatility when trading options. If you check beta on the stock market, you can get an idea of how volatile the stock itself is. A beta larger than 1 is a more volatile stock.

What you really want to keep in mind with implied volatility, is that for a given option, it is going to be affected to variations in the underlying price than one with lower implied volatility.

The Broker

To trade options, you will need to open a brokerage account. This is no different than doing so in order to invest in stocks. You will need some basic information like a bank account, and some brokers might require an ID or proof of address. But it is usually pretty quick and easy. Robinhood is a great broker to use for trading options if you are a beginner, so consider downloading their mobile app.

Picture 3

If you already have a broker, consider using them for trading options. In fact, you are going to use the same broker that you use for stocks in most cases. Mainly what the broker does is facilitate the buying and selling of shares, and in this case they will buy and sell options on your behalf.

If you have a large account, the broker may be willing to lend you money to buy and sell shares or options, in which case you would have a margin account. You are required to deposit $2,000 to open one. Since commissions can eat into profits from options trades, it is important to look for a broker that has low or no commission fees. We have already talked about Robinhood, which does not charge commissions. Besides Robinhood, a good brokerage option to consider is *Tastyworks*. They are focused on trading options and they have low commissions and fees.

Picture 4

Besides any commissions, you will want to know whether or not a given brokerage has a minimum amount of money you need to deposit in your account in order to open trades, and what that minimum is.

The Market Maker

Market makers play a fundamental role behind the scenes when it comes to options trading, and also in other financial markets. These are large players with financial institutions or brokerages that ensure the markets run smoothly.

The truth is you really do not need to know much about the market maker because they operate behind the scenes. What the market maker does, is use their accounts to facilitate trades when there is no actual trader available to buy or sell a contract. They also maintain their own large portfolio.

So, if there was a certain options contract that you wanted to purchase, but there was nobody selling one, in order to keep the market running smoothly the market maker could sell that options contract to you out of their portfolio. The stated goal of a market maker is to ensure that a given market, which in this case is the options market, has sufficient liquidity. This enables traders to buy and sell their positions quickly, meaning you don't have to wait around for a buyer to materialize over an extended time period when you need to get out of a position.

Instead, you could sell your position to the market maker immediately. So, in short, the market maker is a large financial institution that will by contracts to put in their portfolio when there is no willing buyer in the market, or they will sell contracts when there is no willing seller in the market. This all happens behind the scenes, for this reason you are not going to know who or what is actually executing the transaction.

Market makers are people that are contracted to trade on the markets for this purpose. They may work for a financial institution or a brokerage firm. They have to use their own capital in order to participate in the transactions. Market makers have to be very experienced traders in addition to having access to enough capital to take care of the transactions. They will seek to profit from options trades using advanced techniques that we will discuss in the final chapter. These could include spreads and other techniques.

Chapter 3: How Options Prices are Determined

In this chapter, we're going to explore the fundamentals behind options pricing on the market. It's actually fairly easy to predict how the market prices of options are going to change by knowing the expiration date, the price of the underlying stock and a few other details. You can also find options pricing calculators online that will give you the future price of an option for various changes in stock price.

Of course, the fundamental problem in trading, whether you are a day trader, on Forex, or trading options – is estimating future price changes. You can do simple analysis like studying price trends, as well as keeping up with company news including earning reports and product releases, or major announcements such as the departure of a CEO. Any news coming out about a company can cause a major price move, and random trading can cause a lot of ups and downs in price as well, although it takes big news to cause big price changes. The overall economy can have an impact too. If there is a good jobs report, or GDP growth rate, it can send stocks soaring, at least for a short period of time. Of course, the converse is true too, so staying on top of the news helps.

The good thing about options is that since (in most cases) they involve short term deadlines, it makes it a little bit easier to plan. That is, over the course of a year, anything can happen, but, over the next 5-10 days, odds are it will just be business as usual. Of course, you don't want to time an options trade around an earnings call unless you are prepared and have an idea of how it is going to turn out, or unless you have set up a trade to benefit either way.

One of the coolest – and also dangerous - things about options is that there is a direct relationship between the price of the options and the price of the underlying stock. And, it does not take a significant change in the price of the stock to move options prices by a large amount. A $2 change in a stock that is worth $200 is not all that significant, but it can move options prices up or down by as much as $200.

Part of dealing with this is implementing good options strategies to make sure that you don't get nailed by bad trades. Unfortunately, many new traders are not going to be able to get a high designation or high-level trader designation, so they are limited as to the types of trades they can enter. Even so, there are ways around that that we will discuss later. For now, let's just start educating ourselves to find out how options prices are influenced by various factors.

In the Money

Before we get to that, let's review some important market jargon. The first term we need to know is called "in the money." Calls are easier for people to understand because if you are not experienced as an in-depth market trader you are not used to thinking in terms of shorting stocks. Normal people want stock prices to rise. As you learn more about options trading, you will find out that it is not always the best thing. But calls have an intrinsic appeal to that natural belief, thought process, and desire.

A call option is *in the money* when the market price of the stock is higher than the strike price of the option. So, if you have an option with a strike price of $75 and the stock is trading at $80 a share, it is in the money. In short, in the money call options are worth a lot more than options that are *not* in the money. We can take a look at the options calculator to see what the differences can be.

So, I have set up a hypothetical stock which is trading at $80 dollars a share. We will consider an option that expires in 14 days. Just for the record, the implied volatility is 16%, and the risk-free rate is 0.3% (we will explain what that means in a minute).

Setting the strike price at $75 we find that the option (in this case a call) is priced at $5.03. Once again remember that is for a single share, the total price of the option would be $503.

Now let's consider another option with all the same characteristics, but say that this one has a strike price of $70. The price of this option is $10.01, or $1001 to buy the option. The option with the strike price of $70 is also in the money, but it's *more in the money* then the option with the strike price of $75. Another way to express this concept is by saying that it is *deeper in the money*.

If the share price is exactly equal to the strike price, the option is said to be *at the money*. The odds of an option being exactly at the money in the real world are slim, but they can be very close to at the money. These types of options can be of interest because, if the stock price goes beyond the strike, the value of the option can suddenly increase by a large margin.

For a call option, the probability of the share price moving above the strike price can actually be fairly high. Using the example of a strike price at $75, the price of the option would be $0.92 (you would have to pay $92 to purchase the option). If the share price rises to $76 later that afternoon, the price of that call will jump to $1.53.

This kind of price change illustrates why people find trading options so appealing. If you sold right then, that would net you $61 in profit for each options contract.

Out of the Money

When the strike price is higher than the share price on the market, we say that the option is *out of the money*.

Options don't need to be in the money in order to make a profit. Depending on the direction of price movement, you can earn profits from out of the money options as well. We can illustrate this with call options.

If the stock price is rising, the prices of out of the money calls are going to rise as well. So, we shall set up a similar scenario where there are 14 days until option expiration, but, this time, assume that the strike price is $77. Suppose the share price is $75 which is lower than the strike, the option is out of the money.

If the share price rises over the next couple of days, you can actually make a decent profit. The good thing about out of the money options is they are relatively cheap.

Using our example, the $77 strike would cost $0.27 ($27 to buy).

Now let's suppose that, two days later, the share price rises to $76.50. The option is still out of the money. However, the price of the option will rise because the share price is rising. It turns out that under these conditions the price of the option would be $0.66 at that point. That means you could turn around and sell it for $66 when you had purchased it two days earlier for $27.

Many experts don't recommend trading out of the money options. But they remain a great alternative for people that don't have much money to start making profits. This can work if there is a large price move for the underlying stock and you only hold the option for a couple of days. If there is a lot of movement within a single day, you can actually make substantial profits.

Let's consider a real option for Apple. Consider one with the strike price of $220 that expires in 16 days. At market opening, Apple was $192.50 a share. At that time the call option was priced at $0.08: you could have purchased each options contract for a mere $8. Later in the morning, the share price of Apple rose to $195.76. That drove the price of the $200 strike price option to $0.16 (or for all 100 shares, $16). So, we would have an opportunity to double our money, and to make it significant you could buy multiple options simultaneously. Remember to always check the liquidity. Looking at the volume, it is 102 for that option and the open interest is 269. That would be enough liquidity to close the position in a timely fashion.

One thing to remember about options is that if an option expires and it is out of the money, it is also worthless (it "expires worthless"). This holds true for at the money options as well. If the option is in the money at expiration, the price of the option is (share price – the strike price).

How this works for Put Options

A put option works in the opposite fashion, but the concept is the same. When you buy a put option, you will hope to profit off a declining stock price. The concept of *at the money* is the same. So, if the share price is equal to the strike price for a put option, the option is said to be at the money. This is something worth taking note of, as with everything, as you are beginning to work with put options these things might take time to sink in. However, the more you work with it you will get the hang of things, along with making the jargon second nature.

Let us summarize the concepts for both put and call options at the same time. For this situation, we will have a call option and put option both with a strike price of $100.

- If the share price is $100, both the call option and the put option are *at the money*.
- If the share price rises, call options are gaining value, while put options are losing value.

- If the share price is $102, the call option is in the money, but the put option is out of the money.
- If the share price is declining, the value of put options is increasing, while the value of call options is declining.
- If the share price declined to $98, the put option would be in the money, while the call option would be out of the money.

The bottom line is that if you think a stock will depreciate in value or price, then you want to invest in put options. On the other hand, when expecting rising share prices, then the option that would be best to invest in is a call option. It all depends on your analysis of the market and the upward and downward trends of the stocks.

Price of the Underlying

The price of the underlying stock makes up a significant part of the value of an option. Since an option is a derivative based on the value of the underlying asset, which is the stock price, we say that the value of the option due to the price of the underlying asset is called the intrinsic value.

The intrinsic value for a call option is calculated in the following way:

Intrinsic value = price of underlying share − strike price of the option

So, if a stock is trading at $102, and the strike price of a call option is $100, the intrinsic value is:

Intrinsic value = $102 - $100 = $2

That is on a per share basis, so multiply by 100 to get the total intrinsic value for the option.

Variations in the intrinsic value are directly related to the same variations in the share price. If the share price goes up to $5, the intrinsic value of the option goes up to $5. It turns out that there are other factors that influence the price of the option. So, unfortunately, the price of the option itself is only *partially* influenced by changes in intrinsic value. Luckily it does have a large influence. The more in the money the option is, the more the influence of the share price. Also, the influence gets larger the closer the option is to expiration.

As we will see in the next chapter, you can estimate how large the influence is from share price by looking at a quantity called *delta*.

Take note of the below illustration -

Intrinsic value = $0 (when the share price is at or below the strike price)

The intrinsic value for a put option is written in the opposite way:

If the share price is at or above the strike price of a put option, the intrinsic value is zero. If the share price is below the strike price, then a $1 change in the price of the share would affect the intrinsic value of the put option.

Let us consider the following example. Suppose that we have a call option and a put option both with a $100 strike price, both with 5 days left until expiration. If the underlying share price is $98, the intrinsic value of the put option is $2. The price of the put option is $2.61 (per share, so $261 to actually buy). We will talk about time value or extrinsic value below, but the extra $61 comes from the extrinsic value. So, there is $2 in an intrinsic value for all 100 shares, contributing $200 to the price of the option.

The intrinsic value of the call option is zero. However, the call option has the same extrinsic value as the put option, so it is priced at $61.

If the price of the stock jumped to $103, the extrinsic value of the call option would increase to $3. Meanwhile, the intrinsic value of the put option would go to $0.

Both have extrinsic value, which adds to the options prices. The price of the call option would be $3.40 while the price of the put option would be $0.40.

Extrinsic or Time Value

The amount of time an option has left until expiration is priced into the option. This is called *time value* or *extrinsic value*. It is called *extrinsic* because this value is "external" to the value of the underlying asset. The value comes from the fact that any time left until expiration of the option is time over which the market price of the stock can move to a favorable position with respect to the strike price.

The price of the option, in fact, is just the sum of extrinsic and intrinsic value:

Option Price = Intrinsic Value + Extrinsic Value

If the price of a stock is $103 and 5 days to expiration, is going to have an intrinsic value of $3 and an extrinsic value of $0.40

(please note that the values for implied volatility are 30% and we have 0.03% interest rate risk – those will be discussed later).

Intrinsic value (call option) = share price – strike price = $103 - $100 = $3

Option price = Intrinsic value + Extrinsic value = $3 + $0.40 = $3.40

The put option with all items set to the same values is going to have zero intrinsic value, because the intrinsic value of a put option is $0 when it is out of the money. However, the put option will still have an extrinsic value of $0.40, therefore the price of a put option with the same strike price is going to be:
Option price = Intrinsic value + Extrinsic value = $0 + $0.40 = $0.40

You might be wondering why an out of the money option is not worthless. The reason is that there is still time remaining until the option expires. However, the time value of options is always declining as the expiration date approaches on a day by day basis.
If our hypothetical option had 30 days to expiration rather than just 5 days, the extrinsic value would be $2.20 for the call and $2.18 for the put. In that case, the call would cost $5.20 (to buy it $520), and the put option would be priced at $2.18 (to buy it

$218). On the other hand, keeping everything constant but supposing that the time left to expiration was just 3 days, the extrinsic value drops to $0.20 for the call and $0.18 for the put. With only one day to expiration, it crashes to $0.02. The closer you get to expiration the faster extrinsic value drops. We will discuss in more detail in the next section.

So why does extrinsic value decrease like that? Because the less time there is to expiration, the less time there is for the stock to make large moves that would have a large impact on the pricing of the option. At 30 days out, there is a lot of time for the price of the stock to do all kinds of things, so even out of the money options have a significant price from the extrinsic or time value. But as you get closer to the expiration date, there is not enough time for the price of a stock to change significantly (although they sometimes do), and so extrinsic value collapses. On the day of expiration, the extrinsic value goes to zero.

Time Decay

Time decay is a reference to the decline in the extrinsic value of an option as time passes. Extrinsic value is always dropping for any option as it approaches the expiration date. If the option is at or out of the money, at the expiration date, it will expire worthless.

Implied Volatility

Implied volatility influences the price of the option through extrinsic value. High implied volatility means that extrinsic value will be higher as well. The reason is that the more volatile a stock is, the more chance you have that the share price could change. That means that there is a higher probability that the option will end up in the money.

For the sake of an academic example, let's consider doubling and then halving the implied volatility in the previous example. With implied volatility of 30%, we found that with 1 day to expiration, the extrinsic values for the call and put options were both $0.02. If we double the implied volatility to 60% (academic example...) the extrinsic value jumps to $0.30. At 5 days to expiration, it would be $1.59.

On the other hand, suppose implied volatility was halved to only 15%. In that case, at 5 days to expiration, the extrinsic value is $0.04 for the call and $0.03 for the put. At 1 day to expiration, extrinsic value is $0.00, meaning that there is little chance that the share price is going to move enough to make an out of the money or at the money options move to an in the money position. The extrinsic value is only $0.60, as compared to $2.20 and $2.18 for calls and puts respectively if the volatility were 30%.

So, remember that the higher the implied volatility, the higher the extrinsic value of the option is going to be. The lower the implied volatility, the lower the extrinsic value will be.

How many options are exercised

To find out how many options are exercised, we checked with data from the Chicago Board of Options Exchange. According to them:

- 10% of options are exercised
- 30-35% of options expire worthlessly
- 55-60% of options are closed before expiration (that is bought back).

Be sure to keep these numbers in mind if you plan on writing options because it is good to know which percentages are actually exercised. The risk of options being exercised is actually higher than usually presented; it is avoided in practice because experienced traders will buy back options to close out their positions before they are exercised. If you sell to open and the option expires in the money, the broker can exercise the option. Therefore, it is a good idea to buy them back when you sell to open. Of course, remember that extrinsic value drops rapidly as you get closer to expiration, so if you are in a favorable position (for example have written an option that is out of the money as you approach expiration), that means it is going to be cheap to buy it back.

Chapter 4: The Greeks

In the last chapter, we went over some of the factors that influence options pricing. For example, we considered the price of the underlying stock. However, the price relationship between the two is not one-to-one. But you don't need to guess to find out how it is going to change; the relationship between the stock price and the price of the option is something you can look up. The way other properties will change is also tracked. These values are called the "Greeks" by options traders, because they are denoted by Greek letters.

There are four Greeks called *delta*, *gamma*, *vega*, and *theta* that quantify how the pricing of an option is going to vary when the fundamentals change. As we will see in the first section, the "Greek" delta tells us how much the intrinsic value of the option changes when the underlying value of the stock changes by a given point. You don't need to understand how the Greeks are calculated; you only need to know what they mean, so you can look up an option and use their calculated values to make estimates of coming price changes.

Delta

Getting to know the Greeks and what they mean, when it comes options trading, can help you become a more educated and effective trader. A more educated trader is one that is more likely to make profits. So, let's start with the first Greek which is called *delta*. It is also known as the *heads ratio*, but that term is not used very frequently, and in order to look it up you have to find delta.

The concept behind delta is actually pretty straightforward and easy to apply. It tells you how much the price of an option is going to change if the price of the underlying stock changes by one dollar. Consider a delta of 0.68. If the underlying stock changes by one dollar, that tells us that the price of the option will change by $0.68.

The way the Delta changes with time depends on a few factors. Let's take an in the money call option first. When it is in the money, delta increases with the passage of time. The reason why this happens is that extrinsic value is decreasing, while intrinsic value remains directly proportional to the price of the stock. Therefore, delta will increase. At first, this effect is barely noticeable if at all. The less time remaining for the option, the more noticeable it will be.

Now let's consider a call option that is out of the money. In that case, Delta will decrease.

For comparison suppose that we have a call option with a strike price equal to $100. Suppose further that there are 10 days left to expiration. If the underlying stock price is $99 (so that the call option is out of the money) delta is 0.43. On the other hand, if the share price was $101, (so that the option was in the money), delta would be 0.59.

This demonstrates that when the option goes in the money, with all else being equal, it is more heavily influenced by the price of the underlying shares.

To see how this works, let's continue with this scenario. Under the conditions specified with the price of the stock at $101, the price of the call option is $2.54. Suppose that the price of the stock goes up to $102. Since Delta is 0.59, we expect the $1 rise in share price to raise the price of the option by $0.59, to $3.13.

Actually, it raises it a little more, to $3.16, so it was a pretty good estimate. As the price changes delta changes as well. In this case, it jumped to 0.66, meaning that an additional rise in price by $1 will have a greater impact.

Of course, that cuts both ways; delta gives us an estimate of how much the price of the option will drop as well. If we have a value of delta equal to 0.66, we expect a $2 drop in share price to lead to a drop in the price of the option by $1.32. What actually happens is that the price of the call drops down to $1.98, not quite as much as expected. A declining share price means a declining delta, and in this example it drops to 0.51. This implies that the next dollar that the share price drops will have less impact.

When options are at the money, delta will be close to 0.50 in all cases.

For call options, delta is a positive value. It ranges from zero all the way to up to 1.0. The more that the option goes in the money, the higher that Delta will be.

Let's consider our share price at a hundred dollars and suppose instead that we were looking at an option with a strike price of $90. In that case, delta is a very strong 0.98. Therefore, we would expect the price of the option to rise by nearly $1 for every $1 rise in share price. The price of this option under these conditions will be $10.04. Now, if we increase the share price by $1, we find that the price of the option will increase to $11.02. So, the correspondence between the actual change in option price and delta gets stronger, the more "in the money" the option is. Continuing our current example, a strike price of $85 would give us a call option with a delta of exactly 1.0.

If an option is out of money, the closer it gets to expiration the smaller delta gets. In fact, it will quickly go to zero.

Now let's have a look at put options.

For put options, delta is given as a negative value. So, the range for a put option is from zero to -1.0. The meaning is basically the same. It is a negative value because in the case of put options, price movements of puts move in the opposite direction to stock value. In other words, put options become more valuable as stock prices drop.

The negative sign indicates that a *drop* in the price of a share of stock by a dollar is going to cause a rise in the option price - when we are talking about put options.

This means that changes in share price are going to be a little more influential for the option. If a put option is strongly in the money, delta will approach -1.0. Remember that, as the expiration date approaches for a call option, delta goes to zero if the option is out of the money. Put options exhibit the same behavior.

Delta can also be thought of in different ways. For example, it can estimate the probability that an option will expire in the money. So, let's say that you have a call option with the Delta of 0.7. That tells you that there is a 70% chance that the option will expire in the money. Another call option, that had a delta of 0.5, only has a 50% chance of expiring in the money. But remember that delta is dynamic, so that value is only the *probability at this very moment*. A significant change in stock price might change the situation, and one more business day will also impact it.

Another way to look at Delta is in terms of how much money the option will gain or lose when compared to a given number of shares. So, if Delta is 0.8 and the price of the underlying stock rises by a dollar, that means the option will gain as much in price as 80 shares of stock. This is a really smart way to look at things because it shows the power of options. So, you buy one option, but if the price of the stock goes up by $1, you gain the price-worth of 80 shares of stock. Remember that option prices are quoted per share, so to get the full price of the option you have to multiply by 100. Of course, that works the other way as well. If the share price had dropped instead, that would translate roughly into saying that the option lost as much money as 80 shares of stock.

The same relationships hold, but in opposite fashion for a put option.

For in the money options, remember that delta is more influential than it is for out of the money options. We saw that earlier, when we considered different examples, and the in the money option had a Delta that was nearly 1.0. If the strike price is $85 and the share price is $101, then Delta is 1.0. For comparison, if the share price is $101, but the strike price is $107, delta would only be 0.13. It is an out of the money option. That means that an out of the money option is far less sensitive to changes in the underlying share price.

However, if an out of the money option is far from expiration it is also more sensitive to changes in the underlying stock. Let's consider that $107 strike price and move it further from the expiration date. At 20 days to expiration, Delta is 0.22. At 15 days, Delta is 0.18, and as we have seen at 10 days to expiration under the same conditions Delta with the 0.13. So, Delta gets smaller the closer you get to expiration for out of the money options.

The closer an option is to the expiration date, if it is *in the money* the more it will react to changes in the underlying stock price.

Let's suppose that the strike price is $107 and that the share price is $101. That means a put option would be in the money by quite a large margin. At 20 days until expiration, Delta is -0.78. At 10 days until expiration, Delta would grow to be -0.87.

Finally, at five days to expiration, Delta would be -0.95. Don't be thrown off by the negative signs. As you can see, the closer we get to the expiration date, the more strongly our *in the money* put is influenced by changes in the share price.

This tells us that five days to expiration, we would expect a $1 drop in share price to lead to a $0.95 increase in the price of the put option. At $101 a share, the put option would be $6.07. If the share price dropped to $100 that same day, the price of the put option would rise to $7.03. It's not quite an exact match, but it's a very close estimate provided by Delta.

Gamma

Now, let's have a look at the next Greek, which is *Gamma*. This one is a little bit more obscure. Gamma can be thought of as the second derivative if you have experience with calculus. If you have no experience with calculus or you want to forget it, I apologize for the headache.

Basically, what that means is that Gamma gives the rate at which delta will change if there is a one-dollar change in the underlying stock price. As a side note, if you do remember from calculus - a derivative of position with time is speed or velocity. So, you can think of Delta as giving the speed or velocity in the change of price of the option.

Gamma, in this analogy, would be the *acceleration* in the change of the option price. Understanding the details and all the mathematics is not important for most options traders. However, you can keep some basic rules of thumb in mind. The key point is this. *The higher gamma is, the more responsive the option is going to be to changes in the underlying stock price.*

Another way to think of this is to know that Delta changes every time the underlying stock price changes. So, Delta is only as good as the value that we see at a given instance. You can use Gamma to estimate how Delta will change when there is price movement. The further you are from expiration, the higher the Gamma will be.

The more an option goes in the money, the smaller Gamma will get. What that means is that Delta won't be changing as much for a given change in the price of the underlying stock if the option is in the money. If Delta goes to 1.0 then Gamma will go to zero.

Theta

In the last chapter, we spent some time talking about time decay and the extrinsic value. It is a fact that the extrinsic value of an option is going to decrease as time passes. There is simply no way around this. When an option is further away from the expiration date, there are more opportunities for the stock price to fluctuate. This means that fluctuations in the stock price over a longer period of time could put an option that is currently *out of the money*, in the money. As you get closer to expiration there are simply less opportunities for that to happen. So, an out of the money option is not going to have as much value as days pass.

If you just play around with options prices using a calculator or watch them on the markets, it might seem a little bit mysterious how the extrinsic value changes. But you can use Theta to get an idea of what is happening. Theta gives an estimate of how much the price of the option will decrease each passing day. Specifically, it tells you how much the extrinsic or time value of the option will decrease.

Since Theta is telling you how much the extrinsic value is going to *decrease*, it is listed as a negative number. Consider an option with a $50 strike price and a share price of $53. At 15 days to expiration, Theta is -0.027 for a call option, and -0.026 for a put option. Let's look at the call option; the principle is about the same for both. This tells us that the extrinsic value at 14 days will drop by about $0.03. At 15 days to expiration, the extrinsic value is $0.29 for the call option. So, we are going to expect it to drop to $0.26 the following day. As a matter of fact, this is exactly what happens.

Time decay is *exponential* and not linear. If an option is in the money, Theta will decrease in value as the expiration date approaches. If it is out of the money, then it will get larger. This indicates that an out of the money option is going to lose value rapidly, the closer you get the expiration date.

An in the money option will smoothly lose extrinsic value as the expiration date approaches. At the money, options will gain in value as the expiration date approaches. For at the money options, extrinsic value represents a higher proportion of their price as compared to other options. Even though Theta will be smaller for out of the money options, it still represents a greater percentage of losses in price, because extrinsic value represents 100% of the total worth.

In any case, options always lose extrinsic value as the expiration date approaches. No matter where your option is relative to being at the money, in the money, or out of the money, you can take the value of Theta and subtract it from the extrinsic value to determine what it will be the following day.

Vega

Now we are entering territory that is a little more obscure. Vega is related to changes in implied volatility.

So, if there is a one-point change in implied volatility, the implied volatility will alter the extrinsic value of the option. This will be in direct proportion to Vega. Therefore, if Vega is 0.42, that would tell you that if the implied volatility went up one point, the price of the option would go up by $0.42. More volatility means higher option prices. The converse is true as well; if the implied volatility drops by a point - if Vega was 0.42, the price of the option would drop by forty-two cents.

So just remember that Vega would tell you how influential implied volatility is on the price of the option. The higher the value of Vega, the more influential changes in the implied volatility will be on the price. Financial advisors suggest that the best time to buy an option is when Vega is lower than what is considered average or normal. So, if the implied volatility is historically low, that would be an indication that the option is a better buy. On the other hand, if the implied volatility is high in comparison to the historical volatility, that would mean that Vega is higher than normal. This would be a sell signal for the option. But to be honest most options trading does not get that deep in the woods. You will be making your buy and sell decisions based simply on whether you are profitable or not.

More practically, consider that if Vega drops consequently the prices of options will drop. If Vega increases, prices of options will increase too.

Rho

The final Greek that we will look at in relation to options is called Rho. This measures the sensitivity of an option to changes in interest rates. If you pull up an options calculator, you are going to notice that it will include the so-called *safe interest rate* value (or "risk-free"). This is the interest rate that you would receive from the safest possible investment, which is usually considered to be a 10-year US Treasury.

Generally speaking, prices of call options will go up if the interest rate goes up. On the other hand, a rising interest rate would mean a decline in the value of put options. That means that Rho is positive for call options and is negative for put options.

Since interest rates do not change all that much except when the Fed makes a quarterly announcement, it is not really going to be much of a factor in your options trading. Consider that months will go by before there is a change in interest rates (if there is at all), but most options are short-term investments lasting only a few weeks. Generally speaking, options traders are not going to be sitting around worrying about Rho these days. The only time that it *might* be important would be in the case of a LEAP, or long-term option. Even then, it might not matter that much, because the changes in interest rates these days tend to be relatively small. In the near future, if the Fed raises interest rates, the changes are likely to be gradual, and so not have much impact on options pricing.

Chapter 5: Options on Index Funds

In this chapter, we are going to take a brief foray into the idea of buying options on index funds. It is possible to buy options contracts on exchange-traded funds as well as on regular stocks. Buying options on exchange-traded funds is not without risk. However, it can be a little more predictable than doing it for individual stocks. That is because you are simply betting on the direction of the stock market or the price of some major index rather than tracking the fortunes of an individual company.

One of the most popular index funds that is used is called SPY, namely for the S&P 500.

For those who don't know, an exchange-traded fund is basically a mutual fund that trades like a stock. Investment companies collect a large amount of money, and then they buy shares in multiple companies. So, in the case of SPY, the fund owns shares in all 500 companies on the index. A large amount of money has to be assembled to make those kinds of investments.

Try and imagine if you wanted to invest in every single company that belongs to the S&P 500 or the Dow Jones industrial average. That would be quite a daunting task and unless you are a billionaire, it might even be impossible. But you could imagine trying to buy shares in each individual stock. Let's stick with the S&P 500 as an example. That would mean that you would have to pick out the 500 companies and buy shares in each one of them. Chances are not good for you to get very far in this task.

And then you have to take into account that this is not a static list of companies. That is, it will be changing with time. Companies can be removed from the list and new ones added as up and coming corporations replace others.

Another factor to consider would be that you really would not know the best ways to distribute your money among the different stocks even if you had enough to invest in all 500 companies. Usually, investments are weighted so that performance can be improved, as the idea is to beat the market. For this reason, it would be difficult for you, as an individual, to determine how to get the most growth out of your investments.

Therefore, it makes sense to leave such a project to professionals who have a lot of money to invest. So far it sounds like I have made a great argument for a mutual fund. And I suppose that mutual funds do have their advantages. For starters, we know that such funds automatically give you a diverse portfolio. Also, a professional money manager would attempt to build a portfolio with a higher probability of success, there would be a possibility that his or her fund would actually perform better than the S&P 500 index itself. This is in fact, what professional money managers try to attempt with these funds. Instead of putting equal investments in each of the S&P 500 companies, what they will do is put a little bit more money in high growth companies and a little bit less in companies that are stable or even in decline.

Of course, while mutual funds have their advantages for people that are planning for retirement and so forth, they might be boring for people who are inclined to be traders, rather than safety-oriented long-term investors. And there is a good reason for this. One thing to note about mutual funds is that they don't trade on the stock market. They only trade once a day after the market close. Also, mutual funds are well-known for having high expenses. In fact, in case you didn't know, the expenses associated with mutual funds are a bit notorious if they have loads.

Exchange-traded funds were developed with the idea of taking the advantages of mutual funds but without the disadvantages. So, the first major difference between an exchange-traded fund and a mutual fund is that the exchange-traded fund is traded *actively* on the stock market. This is a book about options of course, so we are not going to get into all of the details of why that matters. However, consider the following scenario. Exchange-traded funds trade just like a stock during the day.

So, if the S&P 500 index was going up strongly, you could check the price of the exchange-traded fund, and you may want to get in action. This way you could buy your shares there and then, or at the right moment as the case may be. But you cannot do this in quite the same way for a mutual fund. You could go ahead and submit an order during the day, but your order won't execute until the mutual fund trades at the end of the day. That means you really cannot be sure what price you are going to get. In contrast, an investor buying shares in an exchange-traded fund knows the exact price, just like anyone buying stock live does.

The second major advantage for exchange-traded funds over mutual funds is that they have very low expenses in comparison. So, the cost of investing in an exchange-traded fund as compared to a mutual fund that tracks the same index is going to be a lot lower.

For these reasons, many exchange-traded funds have become very popular. This is an excellent way for people to invest with diversification. So rather than having to deal with some fancy mutual fund with a bunch of polished publications, that are supposed to make you feel good about all the fees that they are charging you, you can simply sign on to your brokerage account and buy shares of an exchange-traded fund whenever you feel like it.

The popularity of these exchange-traded funds has had a big impact on options as well. Before the advent of exchange-traded funds, the only thing you could do with options was to buy them for regular stocks, but nowadays you can buy options in all kinds of different ways and for different types of investments. One of the most popular is the SPY, which we mentioned earlier. If you look at the SPY options, the level of activity as reflected in the volume and open interest is quite large when compared to that for individual stocks.

You may remember the small numbers that we saw with the Microsoft call options. To make a comparison, now looking at calls that expire in two weeks for SPY, we can see that it is slightly out of the money call option had a volume of 13,969 and an open interest of 19,963. That just gives you an idea of the level of activity associated with the options surrounding this exchange-traded fund. There are a lot of people that are trading these options as compared options trading for a lot of regular stocks. There is a good reason for this, and, for you, it means more liquidity, which helps you get in and out of trade quickly.

When you are buying and selling options in this case what you are doing is simply betting on the direction that the S&P 500 will go. Now that will not save you from making the wrong bets from time to time. No matter what, investing is always risky. And when you are talking about the stock market indices themselves, they are going to be more sensitive to external events, such as the government slapping on a new tariff, or if some political event causes an uproar.

This said, remember that, with options, one of the advantages is that we can find profit no matter which way the index moves.

Another great thing about the SPY is that the prices are relatively affordable. The share price of the index fund at the writing time is around $289 dollars a share. This is actually quite a nice price point. So, it is roughly about 10% of what the S&P 500 index is.

It is a good price point because higher prices make it easier to make profits. To make profits on low priced stocks like AMD you have to buy more options, which means less liquidity. At the other end of the spectrum, we have brands like Amazon, which of course is quite expensive, even for options.

So, let's look at a slightly out of the money option that expires in two weeks, so that we can get an idea of what the prices are going to be if we decided to purchase an option. A $289 strike call option which is slightly out of the money, is priced at $1.53. If you remember that options are a hundred shares, which is the price per share, so we could buy this option for $153.

This is a good strategy for when the market is going up. Small changes can mean big money. I, myself, made a recent trade buying some slightly out of the money call options for this exchange-traded fund, SPY. I happened to purchase these options right before a major government announcement related to the general state of the economy. It turned out to be good news, which was pretty much expected, but the actual value was a lot better than what people thought it was going to be. This led to what turned out to be a fairly modest rally in the stock market. Basically, the price of SPY went up by a couple of dollars. If you had 100 shares of SPY, you made a little bit of money. By owning options, however, you would earn $200 per option contract, as I did.

This is a true story, and I hope it encourages you. But, of course, I must warn you that the situation above is far from typical. Nonetheless, those kind of moves are definitely possible when you are talking about an index fund such as this one. It can happen with company options as well, of course. If Apple, for example, had a surprising earnings report that was upbeat and positive, the price of Apple options would probably make a move of a couple hundred dollars.

But one thing about exchange-traded funds that are tracking major indices is that there is more opportunity for things like this to happen. Any good news that comes out about virtually anything that could impact the economy can drive price changes.

Of course, we have to be aware that the opposite is possible too, but that is why a smart investor is a diversified investor. In the case of options that means if you are not using some of these strategies that lead to profits you are at least buying both call and put options, so that you can profit from different price movements. And, obviously, you are paying close attention to what is going on in the world, so that you are ready to sell when necessary.

The thing with options for exchange-traded funds is not just that you can invest in something great like SPY. There are exchange-traded funds for virtually anything under the sun, and since they are listed as stocks, you can trade options on them.

As another example, we can consider the exchange-traded fund GLD. In short, what this exchange-traded fund does is that it allows people to invest in gold. But the difference here is that you are not really investing in gold in the sense of going to buy a bar or nugget that you keep in a safe in your house. Instead what you are doing is buying into a fund that owns interests in gold, but trading it as if it was a stock. Well, actually, of course, the fund itself is a stock.

So, we can trade options on Gold without having to do anything special or go on commodities markets, you can simply do this on the stock market. Now, I haven't personally invested in this one; I am just mentioning it as an example of the variety of investment opportunities that exist when you start considering exchange-traded funds.

Gold is not the only other opportunity that is out there. One interesting twist to investing would be to consider an exchange-traded fund that invested in bonds. There are a wide variety of exchange-traded funds that invest in bonds. One of the most famous of these is JNK. This one actually invests in junk bonds. Now if you don't know what those are, I will briefly say that those are bonds issued by companies that have bad credit. Just like people with bad credit, they have to pay high interest rates. So, imagine if you have bad credit and you try buying a car. You will have to pay a ridiculously high-interest rate. The same principle applies to companies issuing bonds because a bond is the same as borrowing money. So, a company with bad credit is going to be forced to pay high-interest rates on their bonds. So, although there is some risk in principle, you would be earning a really high-interest rate in return for taking that risk with your capital.

The advantage of an exchange-traded fund is that you are covered a little bit by the fact that you are investing in the exchange-traded fund rather than directly in the bonds themselves. So, while a company that may go bust in part underlies the exchange-traded fund, the people that manage the fund are buying and selling the bonds in order to keep the fund performing well. So, you don't really have to worry about some company defaulting on paying their bonds interest payments.

So, this could be another possibility for options trading. Again, this is not something I personally invested in, so I cannot say offhand whether or not this particular fund is profitable. The point of this exercise is to illustrate again the wide diversity of investment opportunities and that exchange-traded funds provide not only long-term investors, but people that might be interested in doing some unconventional business with the options.

Before we close out this chapter, let's look at a few more possibilities. One example is that you can invest in foreign markets through exchange-traded funds. This means that rather than trying to invest overseas, you could buy options on exchange-traded funds that tracked high-growth companies in India or Russia for example. You can do that with conventional investments as well, by looking for exchange-traded funds that invested in real estate or even in US government bonds. The possibilities are basically endless

Personally, I prefer to stick to SPY, when I am buying options on exchange-traded funds, but you will have to study the investment and determine what works best for you and your situation.

Chapter 6: Writing Options and Earned Income

Now we are going to take a look at options from a different angle. Up until this point, our focus has been on buying and then trading options on the market. But there is another way to make money using options if you are somebody who owns shares of stock. And as we will discover, it turns out you don't need to actually own the shares of stock in order to make some money. Although, you will want to keep in mind that some of the possibilities we are going to examine are riskier than others.

If you recall, when you buy an option, you pay a *premium* for it. Now, you have good chances that when you buy an option during your regular trading, you are probably buying it from somebody who bought it from somebody else and so on. But at some point, someone sold to open the option. So, whoever purchased it, from the writer of the option, paid them the premium, which the seller could use as their own income. Selling options can be a nice way to make a good monthly income.

There are a couple of different ways that you can go about doing this. The first way is to actually own the shares of stock that you use as collateral to cover the option. Remember that there is a chance that an option might be exercised. From the statistics that we cited in an earlier chapter, we noted that around 10% of options are exercised. So that possibility is always there. And if you don't own the shares of stock or have money to cover a purchase, it could be a real problem.

Certain people sell options that then they don't even own the underlying stock for, or have the financial backing to purchase shares, and these are called *naked calls* and *naked puts*.

When it comes to selling options, you have to think not only about whether it is a call option or a put, but you also have to consider whether or not it is covered or naked. Either way, the primary goal in most cases is to make income via monthly or weekly payments from selling options. Let's get started by looking at the simplest case, which is a covered call.

Covered Calls

A covered call works in the following way. The seller of the covered call owns at least 100 shares of the underlying stock. People may be speculating that the price of the stock is going to go up. But you can always take a chance if you think that the stock is not going to go up as much as somebody who is trading options is hoping it will go up. Although the price of an *out of the money* call is not going to be the best price that you could get for an option, the fact that it is out of the money cuts the risk that you will lose your shares if someone exercises the option. Secondly, time decay will work in your favor, since as time passes, if the option remains out of the money, it becomes worthless to the buyer. This might seem a bit confusing at first, so let me give you an example.

Suppose that there is a stock that is trading at $100 dollars a share. Consider selling a slightly out of the money call using shares that are already owned to cover it. In this case, we could choose a strike price that is a little bit higher than the market price for the stock right now. For this example, I will choose a $102 strike price with a 30-day expiration date. The price of the option is $2.57. So, if we had 100 shares, we could make $257 by selling the option. If you had 1,000 shares, you could sell 10 options contracts and make $2,570.

But remember there are risks involved in any financial transaction. In this case, the risk is actually fairly low. It is possible that the price of the stock will rise and go above $102, over a 30-day period. And it is also possible that somebody will choose to exercise their option to buy the shares if that happens. Even if they don't, if it goes in the money, the broker can still exercise the option.

Of course, most of the time, stock prices don't fluctuate all that much. But let's say that the price rose to $103. In this situation, it is possible, although certainly not guaranteed, that somebody might exercise the option. If they did so, you would have to sell your shares at $102 per share. But you can buy an option back if necessary as a way to get out of that kind of trouble.

The stock was trading at $100 dollars per share when you wrote the option, so really you are selling the stock at a higher price, and this is not that big of a deal. You are missing out on the $1 higher price that you could have sold the stock at, had you not written the options contract.

However, you sold the option for $2.57. Then you sell the shares for $102, which is a gain of $2 per share. Now add on the $2.57 per share that you got from selling the options contract, and we are up to $4.57 in earnings per share. So, although you lose a theoretical dollar, had you sold the stock on the open market, which brings us down to $3.57, you still made a profit. Of course, we are not taking into account commissions, but overall that won't have that much impact.

When it comes down to it, the actual risk involved is not really selling the stock. Yes, you are giving up a little bit of upside, but you are also still earning money. The real risk is getting in a situation where you are forced to sell shares of stock that you don't really want to sell.

In fact, that is how these options got their name as "calls." The old lingo was that your shares could be "called away" if somebody decided to exercise the option. That is why they are known as *calls*.

In addition to the risk that you might be giving up a future upside, there are other things to consider. If the stock pays dividends, there could be a risk involving the dividend. In simple words, if it is a dividend-paying stock, you have to keep track of the *ex-dividend date*. This is so that you don't get into a situation where somebody exercises their option to buy the shares, and you have to let go of the shares while also giving the buyer the dividend. So, you are probably going to want to look at the ex-dividend date and wait until that date has passed before selling to open against your shares.

Now, in the event that the stock price stays about the same or even declines, then you are in a situation where there is no risk at all. So, using our example if the stock dropped to $99 dollars a share, or even stayed about $100 a share, the option would end up expiring worthless. In that case, you keep the money you earned from the premium, and then you also keep the shares. So, if you are hoping to keep the shares for a long-term investment, then you are all good. You can then repeat the process and earn more premium by writing more options contracts based on the stock.

Some of the things that we can say about this strategy is that it is not the kind of trade that is going to cause you to lose your life savings. The worst thing that could happen is that you may have to sell the shares of stock and miss out on the little bit of profit that you could have made, should the price of the share boost way beyond the strike price. But you are still going to come out ahead financially even though it might not be as good as you could have come out. And you will have to figure out something else to do with the money once you have the shares called away. It is all money that can be reinvested.

Since the risk is relatively low for this type of transaction, brokerages allow level one traders to sell covered calls. For those of you who don't own 100 shares of any stock, unfortunately, that won't be an option for you. But if you do own some shares and you are willing to take some risk in losing the shares, then this could be a way to generate some monthly income.

Some people sell options that expire in as little time as a week because that can minimize the risk a little bit. The reason is that it has less time for the stock to go beyond the strike price and with only a week left on the option, the extrinsic for time value is decaying rapidly.

There are some other possibilities. You can do what is called a close-out. This means that you purchase the call options back, and as a result, your position is closed out. In this case, you might gain or lose money, depending on what the price of the option is at the time you buy it back. But doing this will allow you to retain your ownership of the stock. If the option is still out of the money, it will be much cheaper than you sold it for, so this won't eat into your profits very much.

There is also the possibility of doing what is called a rollout. So, what you do in this case is you buy back the covered calls and then you sell new ones that have the same strike price, but a longer expiration date. So, if you sold covered calls that expired on May 31st, when getting a rollout you would buy them back before they expire and then sell new ones with the same strike price that expired for example on June 30th.

Roll out and up means that you do the rollout strategy, but instead of keeping the strike price the same, you sell the new options with a higher strike price. Conversely, roll out and down is when you use the rollout strategy, but you sell with a lower strike price.

For people who are not too risk-averse, there is also another possibility that of selling call options with a strike price which is actually below the trading share price. Now, why would you want to take that risk? Because the options sell for a much higher price. Let's look at a quick example.

Suppose that your stock is trading at $100 a share. You could sell a call option that expired in 30 days with the strike price of $90 for $10.45 a share. So that would get you a pretty nice premium payment of around $1000 for every options contract that you sold. However, the problem is somebody could exercise their right to exercise the option. That is because the $90 strike price is going to make that pretty attractive when the stock is trading at a hundred dollars a share. So, the risk is real and higher than it would be had you sold a slightly out of the money option. But maybe you are willing to take that risk. For comparison, if you sold it with a $103 strike price, the option would only sell for $2.19, which is definitely less money.

Naked Call

The next strategy is called a "naked" call. This means that you open a position by selling a call that is not backed by the underlying stock. This is a very high-risk move, but it could also be extremely profitable. To sell naked calls, you are going to have to be a higher-level trader, and you are also probably going to be required to have cash in your account because you might need to buy the shares. The risk is that if the option goes in the money and it's exercised, you will have to buy high and sell low.

Suppose that you sell a naked call with an amount of $101 when the stock is trading at $100. Suppose that the company announces they invented a cure for cancer, and the shares jump to $200 a share. In that case, the risk that the option is going to be exercised is going to be pretty high, since a trader could buy the shares from you at $101 a share, which is $99 less than the market price. So, you would be forced to buy the shares at $200 on the market since you did not own them and then sell them to the buyer of the option at $101 a share. An option contract forces the seller to dispose of the shares by selling at the strike amount with no other considerations. So, if you sold one naked options contract in this scenario you lose $99 a share on 100 shares for a total loss of $9,900.

Of course, you will have to weigh everything when deciding whether or not it is worth taking the risk, in most cases, stocks are not going to fluctuate in price as much as we have described here, especially over the limited time periods of most options. So that means there are good chances of you selling naked calls and earning profits from the premiums without much risk of having the option exercised. But it could happen, and you could definitely lose a lot of money.

Most junior traders do not have a high enough level designation to execute this kind of trade, and you will need a large amount of money in your account or use margin. Losses, in theory, could be infinite. So, the "textbook" level of potential losses for this type of strategy, should the stock go up, could grow without limit, but, of course, in the real world they would be capped.

Naked Puts

One of the most popular ways to sell options for income streams is to sell *naked puts*. There are some risks in this strategy, and you have to have a higher-level designation from your brokerage.

First, let's review what a put option entails. A put option gives the buyer the right, should they choose to exercise it, to sell 100 shares of the underlying stock at the strike price. They would use this strategy to make profits if the share price were to tank.

Consider an example. If the strike price of a put option was $50, and the share price dropped to $25, they could purchase the shares for $25 on the market, and then sell them to the writer of the put option at $50 a share. That would earn a $25 profit per share for the buyer. The only hope for the seller of the option is that the stock price rises again to make up the difference so that they can exit the position. Otherwise, they will suffer a huge loss.

However, there are strategies to protect yourself. When you sell options, you have the right to buy them back. So, if you sell a naked put and the stock starts tanking, you can limit your losses by buying them back.

Let's take a specific example. The share price is trading at $100 a share, and you write a naked put with a strike price of $103 with a 30-day expiry. The put is $5.17, so you earn a premium of $517. Let's say at 20 days to expiration, the price of the stock drops to $60 a share. The put option could be exercised, meaning that the option contract owner could buy the shares at $60, while you would be forced to buy them at the strike price, which was $103 a share. This is another example of big losses.

But you could have used a stop-loss order to mitigate your losses. Use the share price to determine your stop-loss order. We could use $95 as an example and suppose the declining stock hit this price with 24 days to expiration. In that case, the option would be $8.56, so we would be losing $3.39 a share. Buying back the options means that we don't have to buy the shares of stock. The $3.39 (per share) loss we have from buying back the options is painful to be sure, but it is still a lot better than having to come up with the money to buy 100 shares at $103 a share when they are only worth $60 a share on the market.

Please note that to sell naked options you must have a margin account, one with enough cash to cover the option as determined by a formula your broker uses. It depends on the price of the stock and the difference between the strike price and the share price. The amount, obviously, is way lower than what you would need to actually cover for the entire option.

Times when naked strategies could work

If the stock price is dropping it is the right time to write naked calls. In a market where stock prices are dropping, the odds are high that any call options written against the stock are going to expire worthlessly. Your profits from the premiums will be smaller, but the risk is also lower.

If the stock price is rising, instead, it is the right opportunity to write naked puts. The risk of the options being exercised in that case is reduced since it's far less likely that the share amount will go below the strike amount.

Besides, options sold out of the money always succeed in raising income without much risk. The trick is selling them far enough out of the money so that your risk is low. This strategy is routinely used by options traders to earn money via naked puts. If the share price starts getting close to your strike price you buy the option back to avoid getting assigned.

Chapter 7: Options Strategies

We are now going to leave the world of selling options and go back to the one that most people are interested in, which is the world of trading options. In this chapter, we are going to have a look at strategies that can be used to increase the odds of profits when trading options. In reality, some of these strategies involve buying and selling options at the same time. Keep in mind that these techniques will require a higher-level designation from your broker. So, it might not be something you can use right away if you are a beginner.

Strangles

One of the simplest strategies that go beyond simply buying options, hoping to profit on moves of the underlying share price, is called a strangle. This strategy involves buying a call option and a put option simultaneously. They will have the same expiration dates, but different strike prices. If the price of the stock rises the put option will expire worthless (but of course it may still hold a small amount of value when you closed your position, and you can sell it and recoup some of the loss). But you will make a profit off the call option. On the other hand, if the stock price declines, the call option will expire worthlessly, but you can make a profit from the put option.

In this case, you can make substantial profits no matter which way the stock moves, but the larger the move, the more profits. On the upside, the profit potential is theoretically unlimited. On the downside, the stock could theoretically fall to zero, so there is a limit, but potential gains are substantial.

The breakeven price on the upside is the strike price of the call plus the amount of the two premiums settled for the options.

If the stock price declines the break-even price would be the difference between the strike value of the put option and the sum of the two premiums paid for the options.

Straddles

When you purchase a call and a put option with similar strike amounts and expiration dates, this is called a straddle. The idea here is that the trader is hoping the share price will either rise or fall by a significant amount. It won't matter which way the price moves. Again, if the price rises the put option will expire worthless, if the price falls the call option will expire worthlessly. For example, suppose a stock is trading at $100 a share. We can buy at the money call and put options that expire in 30 days. The price of the call and put options would be $344 and $342 respectively, for a total investment of $686.

With 20 days left to expiration, suppose the share price rises to $107. Then the call is priced at $766, and the put is at $65. We can sell them both at this time, for $831 and take a profit of $145.

Suppose that, instead of at 20 days to expiration, the share price dropped to $92. In that case, the call is priced at $39, and the put is priced at $837. We can sell them for $876, making a profit of $190.

So, although the profits are modest compared to a situation where we had speculated correctly on the directional move of the stock and bought only calls or puts, this way we profit no matter which way the share price moves. The downside to this strategy is that the share price may not move in a big enough way to make profits possible. Remember that extrinsic value will be declining for both the call and the put options.

Selling covered calls against LEAPS and other LEAPS Strategies

A LEAP is a long-term option, that is an option that expires at a date that is two years in the future. They are regular options otherwise, but you can do some interesting things with LEAPS. Because the expiration date is so far away, they cost a lot more. Looking at Apple, call options with a $195 strike price that expires in two years are selling for $28.28 (for a total price of $2,828). While that seems expensive, consider that 100 shares of Apple would cost $19,422 at the time of writing.

If you buy in the money LEAPS, then you can use them to sell covered calls. This is an interesting strategy that lets you earn premium income without having actually to buy the shares of stock.

LEAPS can also be used for other investing strategies. For example, if Apple is trading at $194, we can buy a LEAP option for $3,479 with a strike price of $190 that expires in two years. If, at some point during that two-year period, the share price rose to $200 we could exercise the option and buy the shares at $190, saving $10 a share. Also, at the same time, we could have been selling covered calls against the LEAPS.

Buying Put Options as Insurance

A put option gives you the right to sell shares of stock at a certain price. Suppose that you wanted to ensure your investment in Apple stock, and you had purchased 100 shares at $191 a share, for a total investment of $19,000. You are worried that the share price is going to drop and so you could buy a put option as a kind of insurance. Looking ahead, you see a put option with a $190 strike price for $4.10. So, you spend $410 and buy the put option.

Should the price of Apple shares suddenly tumble you could exercise your right under the put option to dispose of your shares by selling at the strike price to minimize your losses. Suppose you wake up one morning and the share price has dropped to $170 for some reason. Had you not bought the option you could have tried to get rid of your shares now and take a loss of $21 a share. But, since you bought the put option, you can sell your shares for $190 a share. That is a $1 loss since you purchased the shares at $191. However, you also have to take into account the premium paid for the put options contract, which was $4.10. So, your total loss would be $5.10 a share, but that is still less than the loss of $21 a share that you would have suffered selling the shares on the market at the $170 price. When investors buy stock and a put at the same time, it is called a married put.

Spreads

Spreads involve buying and selling options simultaneously. This is a more complicated options strategy that is only used by advanced traders. You will have to get a high-level designation with your brokerage in order to use this type of strategy. We won't go into details because these methods are beyond the scope of junior options traders, but we will briefly mention some of the more popular methods so that you can have some awareness.

One of the interesting things about spreads is they can be used by level 3 traders to earn regular income from options. If you think the price of a stock is going to stay the same or rise, you sell a put credit spread. You sell a higher-priced option and buy a lower-priced option at the same time. The difference in option prices is your profit. There is a chance of loss if the price drops to the strike price of the puts (and you could get assigned if it goes below the strike price of the put option you sold). You can buy back the spread, in that case, to avoid getting assigned.

If you think that the price of a stock is going to drop you can sell to open a credit spread. In this case, you are hoping the price of the stock is going to stay the same or drop. You sell a call with a low strike price and buy a call with a high strike price (both out of the money). The difference in price is your profit, and losses are capped.

We can also consider more complicated spreads.

For example, you can use a diagonal spread with calls. This means you buy a call that has a shorter expiration date but a strike amount that is higher, and then you sell a call with a longer expiration date and a lower strike price. This is done in such a way that you earn more, from selling the call, than you spend on buying the call for a considerable strike amount, and so you get a net credit to your account.

Spreads can become quite complicated, and there are many different types of spreads. If a trader thinks that the price of a stock will only go up a small amount, they can do a bull call spread. Profit and loss are capped in this case. The two options would have the same expiration date.

If you sell a call with a lower strike price and simultaneously buy a call with a high strike price, this is called a bear call spread. You seek to profit if the underlying stock drops in price. This can also be done by using two put options. In that case, you buy a put option that has a higher strike and sell a put option with a lower strike price.

A bull spread involves attempting to profit when the price of the stock rises by a small amount. In this case, you can also use either two call options or two put options. You buy an option with a lower strike price while selling an option with a higher strike price.

Spreads can be combined in more complicated ways. An iron butterfly combines a bear call spread with a bear put spread. The purpose of doing this is to generate steady income while minimizing the risk of loss.

An iron condor uses a put spread, and a call spread together. There would be four options simultaneously, with the same expiration dates but different strike prices. It involves selling both sides (calls and puts).

Iron Condor

If you think the price of a stock is going to stay within a certain range, you can sell to open an iron condor. This type of strategy requires you to buy a call and sell a call (creating a call credit spread) and buy a put and sell a put (creating a put credit spread). Let's see how it is built in steps. All options in this strategy have the same expiration date.

First, you pick an out of the money call price, a bit above the current share price. You sell this call. Then you buy one with a strike that is a little bit higher. The net difference gives you a credit.

Now you pick an out of the money put option, that is below the current share price. Then you sell this put option. Next, you buy an out of the money put option that has an even lower strike price. The difference here gives you another credit.

The maximum profit is the net credits. The maximum loss is given by (width of strike prices) – entry price. The broker will make you put up enough cash to cover the loss unless you have a margin account.

The narrower you make your strike prices the lower your maximum loss, but the higher the probability that you will experience a loss. The range is set by the two options you sell, you want the stock price to stay within those bounds.

The iron condor is a great strategy to use for monthly income. It can work especially well over short time frames, like a week, since that lessens the chance of the stock going outside the range. However, many traders use a month for their iron condors.

Iron Butterfly

An iron butterfly is another strategy to use if you think the stock price will stay within a certain range. It will use four options, like the iron condor, but there will be three different strike prices.

In this case, you will sell a put option and a call option with the same strike price. The strategy is to get as close to at the money as possible. We will call the strike priced used the central strike. Then you set a differential price we will call x. Now you buy a put option with a strike price of (central strike − x), and you buy a call option with a strike price of (central strike + x).

Like an iron condor, the profit from an iron butterfly is fixed at the net credit when you sell to open. This is given by the sum of the premiums earned from selling the at the money call and put, minus the prices paid for the out of the money options.

The maximum loss is the strike price of the purchased call − strike price of the sold put − total premium.

Conclusions

Thank you for taking the time to read this book and finish it all the way to the end! I hope that you have found it to be informative and educational. Options are an exciting way to get into trading, and the potential is there to make quick profits! To any beginner, things may be a bit too complex with all the jargon that is involved, however, take the time to learn and understand what each concept means and soon things will be much easier. Also, you are here for one purpose, to know how to trade with options and earn profits!

Hopefully, you will take the lessons at heart to mitigate your risks and trade carefully. The first principle to follow in this regard is only to put as much money as you can afford to lose into the stock market. That way, in the event of total loss, you would still be able to go ahead and carry on with your life, and possibly raise more money later to try again.

Of course, with options, it is not necessary to get into a situation where you "lose your shirt," because you can start trading options by only spending a few hundred dollars. This means you can take small risks and build up your account slowly. There are going to be some losses, even the best traders experience losses.

But, if you proceed carefully, you will learn how to trade effectively, and you can rack up more wins than losses.

The best thing to do in order to get started is to buy some calls and puts on index funds. Start small, let your account grow and accept that you are going to have some losses along the way. That is the reality when you decide to work with this type of investment or business – there is a risk for losses along the way. But that does not mean that losses will be a constant thing. If you play your cards right, really study the market and make sound decisions – you are bound to rebound from your losses and start gaining profits. Risk is in everything that we do, and it all just varies depending on how we mitigate these risks and make them work to our advantage. We cannot predict how the market will fare daily, stock prices are affected by a lot of factors, and most of them are things we cannot control, that is one of the things that you need to keep in mind.

If you have found this book informative, please leave us a good review. We love to hear from our readers!

Thank you!

By the same Author:

CURRENCY TRADING MADE SIMPLE
THE ULTIMATE FOREX TRADING GUIDE FOR BEGINNERS
SECRET STRATEGIES, TIPS AND TRICKS

FOREX TRADING

MARK STOCK

SWING TRADING WITH OPTIONS

A COMPREHENSIVE GUIDE FOR BEGINNERS

STRATEGIES TO MAXIMIZE SHORT-TERM TRADING AND MAKE BIG PROFITS

MARK STOCK

Manufactured by
Amazon.ca
Bolton, ON